EXPLORING THEATER

Playwriting

Rita Lorraine Hubbard

Cavendish Square
New York

Published in 2017 by Cavendish Square Publishing, LLC
243 5th Avenue, Suite 136, New York, NY 10016

First Edition

Website: cavendishsq.com

CPSIA Compliance Information: Batch #CW17CSQ

All websites were available and accurate when this book was sent to press.
Cataloging-in-Publication Data
Names: Hubbard, Rita Lorraine.
Title: Playwriting / Rita Lorraine Hubbard.
Description: New York : Cavendish Square, 2017. | Series: Exploring theater | Includes index.
Identifiers: ISBN 9781502622730 (library bound) | ISBN 9781502622747 (ebook)
Subjects: LCSH: Playwriting--Juvenile literature.
Classification: LCC PN1661.H78 2017 | DDC 808.2--dc23

Editorial Director: David McNamara
Editor: Fletcher Doyle
Copy Editor: Nathan Heidelberger
Associate Art Director: Amy Greenan
Designer: Joseph Macri
Production Coordinator: Karol Szymczuk
Photo Research: J8 Media

The photographs in this book are used by permission and through the courtesy of: Cover Hill Street Studios/Blend Images/Getty Images; p. 4 Ray Tamarra/Getty Images; p. 6 alux-um/iStock; p. 11 Anna Jurkovska/Shutterstock.com; p. 16 AIMSTOCK/iStock; p. 18 Geri Lavrov/Photographer's Choice/Getty Images; p. 20 shironosov/iStock/Thinkstock; p. 22 AF Archive/Alamy Stock Photo; p. 25 mediaphotos/iStock; p. 27 John Spence/Shutterstock.com; p. 29 dotshock/Shutterstock.com; p. 35 Christian Bertrand/Shutterstock.com; p. 36 Carlo Allegri/Reuters/Alamy Stock Photo; p. 39 Jason Davis/Getty Images; p. 43 Matt Cardy/Getty Images; p. 44 Juice Images/Alamy Stock Photo; p. 47 Marmaduke St. John/Alamy Stock Photo; p. 51 Alan Wilson/Alamy Stock Photo; p. 53 william87/iStock/Thinkstock; p. 56 Pete Turner/The Image Bank/Getty Images; p. 61 fizkes/Shutterstock.com; p. 66 Steve Debenport/iStock; p. 67 amana productions inc./Thinkstock; p. 70 Walter McBride/Getty Images; p. 73 John Lund/Paula Zacharias/Blend Images/Getty Images; p. 76 pixdeluxe/iStock; p. 78 Per-Anders Pettersson/Corbis Documentary/Getty Images; p. 82 Hero Images/Getty Images; p. 86 SpeedKingz/Shutterstock.com.

Printed in the United States of America

CONTENTS

Theater patrons wait for ticket sales to begin on Broadway.

CHAPTER ONE

CALLING ALL PLAYWRIGHTS

Whether this is your first year in high school or your last, you've probably tried out for many things, like the choir, the glee club, sports, or even the latest talent show. But suppose you're walking down the hallway and you suddenly see a sign posted on the wall that offers a new opportunity. Suppose the sign says, "Calling All **Playwrights**."

Don't laugh. Regional theaters across the United States solicit work from new playwrights every year. They ask for submissions, from **one-act plays** to full productions, and perform the best ones. This is definitely a different and exciting competition. You've probably seen plays before and may have even acted in a few. But you've never written one, so exactly how do you get started?

What's a Play, Anyway?

If you watch television for any length of time, you have an idea of what a play is and how it is structured. The only differences are that television shows are

Some plays are so well-written and popular that they run for decades.

usually recorded in a studio, built around commercial breaks, and shown over and over (reruns) to different audiences—sometimes for generations, as in the case of the *I Love Lucy* television series—and plays are performed in **real time** by live actors on a stage at a theater. Plays can also be watched for generations; *Phantom of the Opera* and *Perfect Crime* had runs that lasted decades.

A play begins with an idea that may have been bouncing around in your head for a long time before you finally decided to pick up a pen or open your laptop to begin writing. This idea can be something that bothers you, like a school fight or a shooting, or something that makes you laugh, like the hilarious things your grandparents say. It can be something you have observed, like how the homeless are treated or how meat is harvested on a farm, or something you have been dreaming of, like going to the prom with the most popular girl or boy, or getting a friend out of a gang. It can be an **adaptation** of something you have seen or read, but you must make sure not to copy someone else's work. It can be short, something like a **sketch** or a one-act play, and it can leave room for **improvisation**. It can be a **monodrama**, but they aren't ideal for school plays because there is only one person in the cast. If the play is a class project, you and your classmates might bounce different topics off of each other and then narrow the ideas down to the best or most exciting ones that you come up with. This is called **brainstorming**.

Once you have a pretty good idea of what your play will be about, you can begin to put it into words. Once you are finished, you will turn it in to the appropriate person (a teacher, a theater director, etc.), and its success will mostly depend upon the collaboration of many participants beside yourself: namely, the director, actors, set designers, makeup artists, and publicity people.

Not Too Fast

Just so we don't get ahead of ourselves, let's go back to the beginning and address some very important questions that must be answered before a play can be written and presented the right way: What skills are needed to be able to produce a play? Do you, for example, need to be a certain age to be a playwright?

Do you need to enroll in any special writing classes to make sure your play comes out just right? Do you need a degree of any kind?

The answer to all of these questions is a resounding no. Playwrights can be any age, any gender, and in any grade, as long as they are old enough to organize their thoughts and put them down on paper.

Some playwrights have earned degrees in English composition, theater, or dramatic literature. Some may have taken specialized courses in **creative writing**, playwriting, or even writing for television or the big screen. Any or all of these courses would be wonderful to have under your belt, but again, they are not necessities. Any elementary, middle school, or high school student can be a playwright. Some preteen and teen playwrights do get some specialized training via writing workshops or community programs, but there's absolutely no penalty if these are not available. A budding playwright can gain experience anywhere: in church plays, by auditioning for school or community plays, or by volunteering at community theaters to get a closer look at how plays are structured. If you are fortunate, you might get to spend some time **shadowing** an experienced actor or playwright.

This thirst for active participation in the theater, along with some good hands-on opportunities like the ones listed above, are good places to start. In short, if you happen to have access to some extracurricular expertise in playwriting, that is good. But if you have nothing in the way of experience except your thirst to write, there's still nothing to worry about.

Tools to Get Started

Most professions have their own unique set of tools to work with. Mechanics use sockets, wrenches, hammers, and more. Artists use pencils, paints, canvases, and brushes. But what tools does a writer need to produce a play?

Many of a playwright's tools can't be touched or held in the hand, but they are just as important as any other tool out there. The American Association of Community Theatre (AACT) offers a list of these playwright tools. They are:

Tool 1: A Vivid Imagination. The fact that you have "the writing bug" is a great start for becoming a playwright, but an even better start would be to have a vivid imagination. Writers with a vivid imagination can "see" different possibilities in their minds. They can "hear" how certain conversations would probably go, and they can predict how people might react to different circumstances.

Where a typical person might see someone sitting under a bridge and think nothing more of it, a writer with a vivid imagination may entertain all sorts of reasons why that particular person is under that bridge. Maybe she's there because she's hiding from someone; maybe she's on some sort of pilgrimage and feels that living in the outdoors is vital to her journey; maybe she is making a statement about what it's like to live under a bridge, so she has vowed to spend the next thirty days and nights living under different bridges.

Whether the person under the bridge is an alien that has come from another galaxy to study human life, or whether she is simply a person under a bridge and nothing more, the point is that a person with a vivid imagination can create many scenarios from this one instance.

Tool 2: A Gripping Idea. The second most important tool you need to become a playwright is an idea. You must have something to write about. Think of something that's important to you, such as a childhood memory, a routine you hate (or love), or some type of political or personal movement that has had an effect on you.

You might decide that some specific cause or "bucket list" of fun destinations should be the subject of your play. Or you might even consider writing about someone whose life and experiences have inspired you, like a paraplegic who finishes the Boston Marathon, or a teen-preneur whose invention is raking in millions. Whatever moves you, whatever inspires you, whatever fires your imagination—that's the subject you should consider turning into your play.

Tool 3: Knowing What Makes People Tick. For your play to be realistic, you must know what makes people "tick." In plain language, this means you must know how and why people say what they say, do what they do, and react the way they react. What are their motivations? To learn this, you must watch people, ask questions, research people and situations (if you have time), and most important of all, *listen* to people talk.

Have you ever heard the old nursery rhyme about the wise old owl?

Listening to and observing people is the best way to learn about human nature.

There once was an owl that lived in an oak.
The more he heard, the less he spoke.
The less he spoke, the more he heard.
Why can't we be like that wise old bird?

—Author unknown

This may be a fun (and rather childish) rhyme, but it is spot-on when it comes to learning what makes people tick. Understanding other people will mean putting yourself, your thoughts, your opinions, and your experiences aside and listening to others tell you about their lives, how they reacted to different things, and what their experiences have been. Encourage others to tell you what motivates them, what scares them, what excites them. If you speak at all, it should be to ask questions to get answers that fill in any gaps that might exist in the information you've gathered.

For example, let's say you have decided to write a play about a teen who wants to go to the Olympics. To understand the thrill, excitement, and wonder of going to the Olympics, it's best to get the description straight from the mouth of a person who has actually been to the Olympics. This would mean speaking to someone via telephone, email, or Skype, or if none of these are available, watching a video interview on YouTube or any other video site.

Tool 4: Knowing How People Talk. Whether you are writing a play or a novel, one of the most important ways to convey information is through **dialogue**—and you definitely want that dialogue to be realistic. Here is an example: Let's say your fourteen-year-old main **character (protagonist)** is late entering the classroom and a teacher immediately begins to yell at him. Your character's eyebrows turn down as he says …

Allow me to offer my apologies, but I was detained for a period by my previous professor. (Unrealistic)

Sorry, my last teacher kept me after class. (Realistic)

See the difference? Both sentences mean the same thing, but only one is realistic because most people don't use formal English, especially teenagers, when speaking. They are typically more informal in their dialogue.

What this all means is that you need to learn to listen to the way people speak so that you know what "natural" dialogue sounds like. You can do this by listening to conversations on the school bus, in the cafeteria, at church, in the gym, or even in your kitchen at home. Try it! Listen to how formal or informal people are when they talk to each other. Note whether they begin each sentence with the other person's name, or whether they leave the name out of the sentence as the conversation goes on. Do they interrupt each other's conversation? Do they use a lot of "Uhs" and "Ums"? Modeling your dialogue off of the way real people speak should do wonders for your play. These rules also apply to **monologues**, which are long speeches by one character.

Tool 5: Understanding the Elements of Dramatic Structure. To write a play, you must know how a play is structured so you can develop a **plot**. A play has at least five elements:

Exposition (backstory). This is the part of your story that introduces the "who, what, when, where, and why" of your play, informing your audience who the story is about, what's happening in this person's life, why this situation or event is happening, and where and when the story takes place (the **setting**).

Rising Action (conflict). This is the series of events that begins happening immediately after the backstory is established. This could be anything from the main character's mother getting sick to the character being bullied by an **antagonist** or having to move with his or her family to a new city, and thereby, a new school. These "happenings" set up the **climax** and resolution of the story.

Climax. The turning point in the story, this is the moment the stakes are at their highest. It's the moment that changes everything for the main character, the moment that tests the character's love or courage or imagination, or whatever the issue might be. For example, if the character has been bullied all throughout the story, the climax might be the point at which the character decides to stand up to the bully once and for all, regardless of what may happen.

Falling Action. Falling Action is the "moment of final suspense" in which the main character either wins what he or she has been striving for, or loses it.

Resolution. This is the **denouement**, or the moment when the quest is over, the **conflict** (whatever it may be) is resolved, and life goes back to normal for the main character.

Tool 6: A Basic Understanding of Nonverbal Expression. There are times in any play when words are not used or they are simply not necessary. In these cases, the actors may be doing something physical onstage, like dancing, marching, painting, or sewing. Other times, words are unnecessary because the actors use facial expressions (a smile, sniff, wink, salute, or any other type of movement) to get their message across. Or they may use gestures, like waving, shrugging their shoulders, or beckoning. When you think of nonverbal communication, think of mimes. They are the masters of nonverbal communication, using their faces, hands, and entire bodies to get their point across. However, you must provide the actors with verbal clues in the dialogue so they understand what they are saying with their bodies.

Discipline Required

Writing is hard work, so one of the main skills required in a playwright is the ability to sit down on a regular basis and write. This is not a sometime thing. You need to be able to schedule regularly long periods of time to write when you will not be interrupted. This means that you will have to turn down invitations from friends if they ask you to do something during a scheduled writing time. The more you write, the better you will get at it. If you are too easily pulled away from writing then you might not have the temperament to be a writer. You also need to be able to tell a story. You can practice this on friends by relating things that happened in the shortest way possible then asking them to tell you what they think happened. If their version matches your version, then you have the talent.

This is a lot of information to digest before you even pick up your pen or open your laptop to begin writing, so please know that you are not expected to learn all of it overnight. You should simply use the information as a guide as you prepare to pen your very first play. Good luck!

Writing a play may seem daunting, but everything will begin to fall into place.

Checklist: What You Should Have Learned

You must have a story to tell.

You should have a great imagination.

You should know the elements of dramatic structure (how a play is structured).

You must learn how people talk to each other.

You should know what makes people tick.

Don't worry about having any type of formal education or qualifications to write your play. After all, you're still in school, so chances are you haven't had the opportunity to pursue any degrees or two-year certificates.

Use every opportunity to think about what type of play you want to write.

CHAPTER TWO

WRITING THE PLAY

Now that you know what it takes to write a play, the next step is deciding whether you're up to the challenge. If your answer is yes, here's how to get started.

First, you must realize that writing a play—or writing *anything*, for that matter—involves both mental and physical action. The play itself is the end result, the final product you want to offer to your classmates, family, teachers, friends, and community. However, this final product doesn't just appear out of nowhere—and it doesn't happen overnight, either. You have to carefully construct your story, and this construction usually begins with preparatory activities like thinking and brainstorming.

Thinking

If you asked a dozen writers how long it took them to write a script or a book, each would give you a different answer because there is no set timeline on writing and finishing a project. However, it's a safe bet that they would tell you that they spent weeks, months, or even years just thinking about their script or book before they actually began to write.

When a writer's script or book is in the prewriting stage, nonwriters won't see anything happening, but you can bet that plenty is going on. The writer may be tweaking characters, deciding on the **setting** or time frame, or even settling on how long the project will be. He or she may be deciding on character strengths and weaknesses, or may simply be hearing conversations in his or her head that will be put down on paper.

By the way, try to keep yourself ready for a creative flash by having your pen and paper with you at all times. Better yet, keep some sort of recorder nearby, if you have one. The recorder can be a stand-alone device, or it could be a recorder app on your cell phone. Either way, keep it handy so that if you're walking down the hallway and an idea hits you, you won't have to pull out pencil and paper and find somewhere to write. Or if you wake up in the middle of the night with an excellent idea, you won't have to stumble about in the dark trying to find pencil and paper.

Carry something to record great ideas.

You probably won't have a year to come up with a play, or even a few months, but whatever amount of time you have, you will almost automatically begin bouncing things around in your head. You may be mapping out fight sequences or choreographing dance moves. You may be staging a kissing scene or plotting a tear-jerking moment when your character visits his or her sick grandmother. You may even be thinking of the type of music that would be perfect for the production.

All of this activity is part of the preparation process. Sooner or later, depending upon how much time you've been given to submit a draft, you will have to move from mental energy (thinking) to actually jotting a few ideas down. That's where "brainstorming" comes in. You will brainstorm ideas of how you want the story to unfold, who will tell it (the main character), and what the outcome will be.

Brainstorming Alone

To brainstorm is to produce an idea or way of solving a problem by holding a spontaneous creativity session. When people hear the word "brainstorm," they naturally think of a group of individuals bouncing ideas off of one another, but it doesn't always have to be this way. It is entirely possible to brainstorm alone; people do it all the time when they must come up with a solution to a problem and they think about the problem from every angle until they figure things out. Since you are working on your first draft, it's probably best that you brainstorm alone this first time and get your story onto paper before you begin asking for other people's opinions about your story.

Gearing Up to Write

On Your Mark

Sooner or later, the information, ideas, and conversations swirling around in your head will need to be put onto paper. This is called writing your first draft. Here are the tools you'll need to help the process go smoothly:

- Your idea
- A pen and some paper, or
- A laptop
- A quiet room for brainstorming alone (i.e., the library, your bedroom)
- A vivid imagination

As you lift that pen or as you turn on your laptop, keep the following thought in mind to help your writing proceed as smoothly as possible:

Your Character(s) May Take Over. You may find that although you had one intention for your character or story, the character seems to take over the story and tell it the way he or she wants it to be told. This happens to

Some characters have a will of their own and can take over a story.

many writers and is perfectly normal. For example, let's say you have a character who never speaks up, especially when he's being laughed at. Maybe you've decided that he will never speak up in the play, but as you write, you suddenly and unexpectedly write a scene where he not only speaks up but also dares anyone to say another word about him. When this happens, you are in tune with your character and are allowing him to tell his own story. This is entirely normal.

Get Set

Here are two brief steps to kick-start the writing process:

1. **Decide.** No matter how many great ideas you came up with as you were brainstorming alone, you can only use one. It's time to decide which idea you will use.
2. **Outline**. Use the following outline to put your ideas into some sort of order:

   What is the title of your play? If you don't have one yet, write a temporary title.

   What is your story about?

   Who will tell your story? Who is your protagonist (leading character)?

   Does the protagonist have a funny name? A unique facial expression?

   Does your protagonist have a best friend?

   Does your protagonist have a nemesis (rival or archenemy)?

What does your protagonist want?

What's stopping your protagonist from getting what he or she wants?

What happens first in the story?

What happens next?

What happens last?

How does the story end?

Write

It's time. This is the moment when you write your play from start to finish. No matter how much a typo may beg you to correct it, ignore it. Why? Because this first draft isn't about perfection, it's about getting the story down on paper. You can tweak the finer details once you're done. The fact is, it is too easy to get gridlocked in editing, tweaking, and revising your writing before you have even made any significant progress. Therefore, it is strongly suggested that you switch off your inner editor and just write.

Your inner editor is that urge writers have to keep checking and rechecking what they've just written for typos before they move to the next line or paragraph. This urge compels the writer to spend way too much time perfecting a sentence, paragraph, or page instead of getting the story down on paper. This not only wastes valuable time, it may also leave the writer depressed and feeling that he or she is making no progress because he or she has not produced more than a paragraph or two.

Turn off your inner editor and get your complete play down on paper.

Don't let this happen to you. Don't worry about spelling, punctuation, or even format. Just write.

Keep going until you get to the end of the play. Then and only then should you look to see what you've created. It may be a wordy mess or it may have a lot of merit. It doesn't matter which it is, because the bottom line is, it's a start.

First drafts are rarely anything to brag about. That's why you need patience and perseverance when you write your play. You'll need it as you tweak the storyline, characters, scenes, and dialogue.

After the First Draft

Now that you've completed your first draft, you can breathe a sigh of relief, right? Wrong. The tweaking/revising stage is just as involved as the draft stage. Here are the steps to help this stage proceed smoothly toward a polished stage production:

Edit

The revision stage is a type of analysis stage. This is the point where you read over what you've just written and decide what's good, what's bad, and what's missing from the script. It's the stage where you will blend in all the elements, characteristics, and scenes that you may have overlooked in your first draft.

If possible, print out what you have written and read it out loud. Or better yet, have some friends read it out loud so you can listen and determine how things sound, whether they make sense, and what definitely needs to change. Things that make sense to you while you're writing often come out a garbled mess when they are read aloud, meaning they will probably not make an ounce of sense to anyone else who reads the play.

This is one of the most important reasons that you need patience when you're revising. It takes patience to get from a mess to a polished script. By the way, now is the time to delete all unnecessary words, phrases, and paragraphs that don't do anything to move the script forward. Moving the script forward means adding information that is crucial to the audience's understanding of a character or an event that will lead them to the play's resolution. You're probably wondering if it will be hard to slice away your precious words after you've worked so hard on your play. The answer is yes, it will be hard. However, it's very necessary in order to get to the meat of your script.

Rewrite!

Now that you've edited your script, it's time to rewrite. This is probably your most crucial step

Get friends, family, and classmates to help you analyze all the parts of your play.

before you begin to stage your play. You will need to assess your play and decide whether you have included all the scenes the audience needs to see to understand the storyline. You'll need to make sure the dialogue makes sense based on the plot, and whether it seems realistic. You'll need to make sure that all of your stage directions—verbal and nonverbal—are clear, and that the actors will be able to do them. You'll also need to assess your setting and make sure that you've described it well, and that your audience knows where and when the story takes place. You must make sure the vocabulary and actions match the time and place of the story. As an example, if the play takes place in the 1960s, don't have a character change the television channel with a remote. People then had to get off the couch and physically change the channel. Introducing a remote to the 1960s would be an anachronism.

This is the time to make sure you know what your main character wants, because if you don't know what your own character wants, your audience certainly won't. You should also make sure your characters are different from each other and have their own peculiar "**tags**" to help the audience tell one person from another. A tag is a physical or verbal way of doing things that the character does consistently. It's the way a person acts, speaks, walks, combs their hair, or does other things that are unique to him or her. The tag could be a sniff, a snort, a twitching eye, a high-pitched giggle, an exaggerated limp, or something as simple as the character constantly wiping his or her glasses clean. The tag should reveal something about that person.

You will need both patience and imagination as you move through these steps. Perfecting a play or any other type of manuscript rarely happens on the first try. It often takes hours, days (including weekends!), and sometimes months of writing and rewriting to get the story just right.

It also takes collaboration with readers, actors, or cowriters (if you write as part of a team) to make sure that your true meaning shines through. This is the point in the process where you should solicit opinions from your friends and family, and where you'll do your brainstorming as part of a team instead of on your own.

Becoming a Team

Now that you've finished your first few drafts, it's time to remember that you were never meant to do this alone. It is now time to bring in friends, classmates, or family members to help you determine your play's strengths and weaknesses.

During this stage, you should meet with some fellow classmates, writers, or playwrights and get their thoughts on your play. You can hand out copies or someone can read the play aloud to the group.

Don't go it alone. Pull a brainstorming team together and watch the ideas roll in.

Either way, you should encourage the group to tell you which parts seem crystal clear, which parts are confusing, and which parts simply don't work.

Keep in mind that critiques, criticisms, and opinions can hurt. Sometimes people are trying to be helpful, and sometimes they're trying to be downright cruel. Try not to get too upset by what others say. Just pick out the jewels—the good things you can use—and allow those to help strengthen your play.

Now that you know what friends, classmates, or fellow playwrights think of your play, it's time to engage in a little—or a lot—of brainstorming. As mentioned, to brainstorm is to produce an idea or way of solving a problem by holding a spontaneous discussion. In this case, it is a group discussion in which one person's idea kicks off another person's idea, which inspires another person's idea.

Here's an example of brainstorming a science fiction idea using the earlier suggestion of the old woman under a bridge. You might begin the brainstorming session by exploring some of the reasons this woman might be under the bridge in the first place. Maybe she's just a homeless old woman with no family that cares. Maybe she broke out of an old folks' home and is the subject of an APB (all-points bulletin). Maybe she's an alien disguised as a bag lady, and she has camped under the bridge to observe earthlings and possibly take a human back to her planet. Or maybe she's a billionaire undercover boss who has pledged to give a million dollars to the first person who shows an ounce of kindness and compassion toward her. See how much flair a brainstorming session can add to an otherwise ordinary storyline?

No two people (or teams) brainstorm alike, but there are some very easy and effective steps that can be taken to help kick-start the process:

1. If you don't already have one, pull a team together. Ask some of your friends, family members, or even associates who happen to like writing or playwriting to join you in the brainstorming session.

2. Lay down some rules. For example, tell the group that everyone's ideas are welcome and no suggestion is stupid or useless. Charge the group to not make anyone who offers a suggestion feel awkward, silly, or uncomfortable in any way.

3. Explain the topic and tell what types of tips or suggestions you're looking for,

otherwise the conversation will probably be all over the place. There is a great example of how conversations can go all over the place in the football movie *The Replacements*, starring Keanu Reeves. In this movie, the coach asks the team to talk about what they are afraid of. The coach is referring to what they (the players) are afraid of on the football field, but because he didn't make this question clear, one of the players says, "spiders," and another one says, "bees." It takes a moment for the coach to bring the conversation back on track. Don't make this mistake. Be specific from the beginning.

4. Set a time limit for brainstorming. Sometimes when you fail to put a time limit on a task, people think they have lots of time to do it so they procrastinate and it never gets done. Tell your group that the brainstorming session will last only fifteen or twenty minutes (or whatever time you decide). Even if you decide to accept suggestions the next day or even the next week, your team will know that the major brainstorming session will begin and end at a certain time and they won't feel the urge to procrastinate.

5. Designate someone to take notes. Someone needs to write down all the brilliant ideas. It's OK if it's you, but

sometimes it's best to have a second writer to take notes. This leaves you free to focus only on the ideas that spring from the session.

6. Look over the ideas. Discuss the ideas with the group. Figure out what can and can't be used, then get started on writing your draft idea, and so forth.

Back to the Drawing Board

If your critique and brainstorming sessions went the way they were supposed to, you should have received enough feedback and fresh ideas to revamp your script. Here's what you should do next:

Revise Again. It's time to reshape your play. By now, you should know who and what your play is about, what happens to him or her, and why the audience should even care. All of these elements should be emphasized as you work with your script. Plan to read your play aloud to your family, friends, or classmates to get their opinion of whether it is clear and makes good sense. This will also be the time to discover whether your critique group's suggestions actually help your play.

Stage It. What sounds good on paper may not make a bit of sense when it's acted out on the stage. It may not even be able to be done. You will eventually do a walk-through of your play with the director, but at this point, you need to do one alone. See if what you've envisioned in your head is possible on the stage. You can rewrite scenes on the spot. Later, be sure to chat with the director about your scenes and what you feel is needed to bring the play to life.

Tweak It! As you stage your play, be sure to jot down notes and details so you'll always know what works and what needs fixing. For example, maybe you have ten characters dancing, but when you stage it, you discover that the stage is too small and the scene will likely end in total chaos. You might make a note to cut the number to only five dancers instead of ten. How else can you tweak your play? Ask yourself:

1. Does my play have a beginning, middle, and end?

2. Have I written all the scenes that are needed to tell the story? Are there any words or actions that are not explained by something mentioned earlier in the script?

3. Will the audience be able to tell who the main character is and what they want or need (main conflict)?

4. Can the audience identify with my characters? In other words, are my characters believable, or are they unbelievable?

5. Do I have enough dialogue?

6. Have I made each character stand out, or do they all seem alike?

7. Do the characters change by the end of the play? For instance, if the character is immature

or a bully, does he or she change mentally, emotionally, or physically by the end of the play?

This is not an exhaustive list. There are probably many more questions you can ask yourself as you tweak your play. Continue to add to this list as questions or situations arise.

Submit It. By now you've put a lot of work and sweat into your play. You've imagined, outlined, brainstormed, and written up a storm. You've hoped and dreamed and put your very best into your play. But you're still not finished. Why? Because you still need to submit it.

Hall of Fame ice hockey player Wayne Gretzky once said, "You miss 100 percent of the shots you don't take." Loosely translated, it means you can't score if you don't shoot. If you don't take your best shot, if you don't at least submit the play and wait to see what happens next, you'll never succeed. So go ahead. Submit your play, wait for your teacher or theater director's feedback, and hope for the best.

Checklist: What You Should Have Learned

It may take you a while to think out the details of your play.

Use a checklist (sample included) to help you organize your play.

Try to get inside your character's head to make your play more realistic.

Stage your play with the director to determine the best blocking for your characters.

Write your play all the way through without stopping.

Turn off your inner editor until your first draft is written.

First drafts are rarely ever perfect, so be prepared to tweak and revise.

Take some time to read your play aloud to see if it makes sense.

It's best to get a critique from friends to get different perspectives.

Brainstorming with others can help to make your play better.

Do a walk-through of your play to see if you've staged it correctly.

You've done all the hard work. Now submit your play!

Get to know the production team that will help bring your play to life.

CHAPTER THREE

WEARING MANY HATS

Naturally, until you actually write your play, there is no need for a production staff of any kind. Why should a team come together when there's nothing to produce? Therefore, all theater roles are dependent upon you, the playwright, to put your play down on paper, even if it isn't perfect at the time. Then comes the great news. You submitted your play, your teacher or theater director loves it, and they have decided to stage it.

Now the rest of the team can spring into action. It is time to assign a director, audition actors, and prepare for production. But what is your role in this stage of the process? Since your part (writing the play) is finished, does this mean you're not needed? Should you go home and stay there until the play is ready to be performed, or should you show up in case there are questions? Exactly what is expected of you now that the writing part is over?

If you had written a script for television or the movies, your role would indeed be over. However, because this is high school, there's plenty for you to do. There are three major stages in the production of the play: preproduction, rehearsal, and performance.

Specific steps must be taken during each stage. This will help you understand your role in each of them.

Preproduction

"Pre" means "before," so the preproduction stage is the work that is done for and on the play before rehearsals even start. The best way to begin that work is through concentrated teamwork.

At this point, you have already engaged in a bit of teamwork. This happened when you solicited friends and family for a script critique and a group brainstorming session. Now you will be working with a team that has a common cause: putting on your play. This team can be large or small, but whatever its size, each team member works interdependently with the others on a specific job, assignment, or task to help reach the desired outcome. In other words, everyone on the team has a part to play, and the end result (in this case, a successfully produced play) will only happen after everyone has done his or her part.

In theater, teamwork is necessary because there are many roles involved in developing, staging, and producing a play, and if the final product (the play) is going to be successful, the people involved need to work together. What happens when people don't work together? Chaos, that's what. Here's an example: Have you ever called a department store to ask a question, only to be transferred to a different department, and then another—and every employee you spoke with gave you a different answer? You probably ended up explaining the same thing over and over again to everyone you talked to, but after who knows how

This quartet works together to produce the best sound it is capable of making.

long on the telephone, you still didn't receive an answer to your original question. Frustrating, right? This is what happens when teamwork breaks down or is nonexistent. Although everyone is supposed to be working together, no one knows what the other person on the team is doing, so nothing productive ever happens.

If your play is going to be successful, you'll need everyone involved on the team to be on the same page. Being on the same page simply means that everyone must be aware of what the task is, what each team member is expected to do, and what each team member expects you to do to complete the task. Think of it like a job description: everyone's role is spelled out from beginning to end so that one person's role does not overlap with another's role and no necessary step is left undone.

FINDING A PASSION

Amara Miranda Jean Brown is a creative writer who grew up auditioning for neighborhood plays. She landed her first part at age seven, and by high school she had acted in several plays and was even trying her hand at writing. She attended the Chattanooga High Center for Creative Arts in Chattanooga, Tennessee, a school that claims to "develop the academics and artistic abilities" of its students by offering the opportunity to explore their gifts and talents. She joined the Speech and Drama League, where she was allowed to choose her own pieces to perform.

By graduation, Amara was thankful for her time in the theater but decided that acting was "hard and time-consuming." However, when one of her teachers told her about playwriting, she knew what she wanted to do. She began writing, entered a few area and national competitions, and began receiving recognition for her raw writing talent. In 2016 she was in her fourth year in college as an English and creative writing major, and had been accepted into a six-week TV screenwriting course. Amara's advice for emerging playwrights: "Take as many classes as you can. Writing plays is like writing any paper. You think it's good, but it's not. It's just not. I recommend pursuing higher education courses in theater and purchasing as many books as you can on the subjects of playwriting and theater."

For example, what would it be like if everyone on your theater team insisted on being the one to approve the costumes the actors will wear, but no one wanted the responsibility for handling the cue cards or other prompts? If someone forgets his or her lines on opening night and no one is manning the prompts, this could stall the play and force other actors to get out of character to try to help the one who forgot his or her lines, or to **ad lib** or improvise. This could, in turn, jeopardize the production, cause a mountain of embarrassment, and almost certainly lead to disaster. Or what if everyone insisted on being responsible for the audio (sound), but no one wanted to be responsible for the lighting? Not only would the audience end up squinting through the darkness to figure out what is happening on the stage, but the people on the stage might actually be in danger of injuring themselves because they cannot see where they are going. It wouldn't take long for the audience to become annoyed and head for the exits.

Team Roles

To understand teamwork in the theater, you must understand all the roles that are involved in producing a successful play, how they depend upon each other to get the job done, and how you, the playwright, will interact with each.

Once you have written your play and it has been accepted, it is time to bring in an actual producer to serve as a sort of project manager. The producer first reads your script to get an idea of the story you want to tell, how many actors you'll need, what sort of props you'll need, and how many sponsors are needed to raise the necessary funds to make the production successful. Then he or she moves into action and "makes the production happen." The producer makes it easier for you to focus on your script and leave the other details in his or her capable hands.

One of the supporting staff members your producer will recruit (if the producer doesn't serve in the role) is a director, who interprets your script based on the dialogue and stage directions you've written, and on what he or she feels that you (the playwright) are trying to say, and does the **blocking**. He or she typically holds auditions to find actors for the various parts and decides how a scene should be played and how the actors should speak, move, and project their lines to the audience. As the playwright, you will probably be asked to be present at the auditions since you wrote the play and had certain characteristics in mind for the characters when you wrote the parts.

The actors are the people who will play the roles of the characters you have created. They are the ones who will bring your play to life. They should have a clear vision of who their character is and what their character wants.

Once the actors are on board, costumers and makeup artists will be needed to make the actors look more authentic. These are probably art or design students who love to paint, draw, sew, or express their creativity in other forms. The costumers will make, rent, or revamp a costume for the production. In turn, the makeup artist will apply makeup or a special prosthesis (such as a hump on the back; a long, crooked nose; a face mask; etc.) to actors before they go onstage.

Stagehands take their team roles seriously and want your play to be a success.

As you and the director stage the play, the set designers and stage hands (who typically work backstage, or behind the scenes) will create sets by building, painting, or procuring the props (chairs, beds, tables, etc.) to create the illusion of a room, restaurant, or building. They are the ones who will move or arrange the furniture, paint the scenery, change the backdrop, or physically move or set up the scenery, lights, microphones, speakers, props, rigging, and other special effects.

While everyone else is racing to get all this done, a printer/graphic designer will design the posters or flyers for the production. The producer is in charge of finding and paying the designer. The design may include original artwork or lettering, or it may be made from an existing template. It will tell the public the name of your play, when and where it will be performed, who will star in it, what time it begins, and how much the tickets will cost. After the design is finalized (possibly by you, the producer, and the

The ticket seller is vital to your team because she helps get people into the theater on time.

director), the printer/graphic designer sees to it that posters, flyers, and even theater tickets are printed and ready to be distributed. He or she would be responsible for proofreading the material for errors and making sure the final product is typo-free, legible, and colorful, and that it includes clear instructions on when the play is happening and where to purchase tickets.

Once all of this is done, he or she will make sure the final product gets into the hands of the **publicity person** (if you have one), who will swing into action and send out PSAs (public service announcements) to the newspapers and radio stations, and to post them on Facebook, Twitter, and other local and virtual bulletin boards. He or she will also send posters and flyers out to be placed in nearby store windows and on bulletin boards.

Ticket sales may be handled by the publicity person or by a separate sales department. The person or persons responsible for sales will distribute tickets to buyers for a price and/or collect tickets at the door. They will keep a tally of the exact number of tickets that have been distributed for sale, the exact number that have been sold, how much money has been collected, and how many tickets remain unsold.

Action Intensifies

Now that you are acquainted with the team of people who will work together to produce your play, it's time to find out what you must do before seeing your play performed before an audience.

Before any actors are chosen, you should give the producer a thorough explanation of your vision for the play and talk about your ideas for the sets, props, and layouts that you feel are necessary to make the play work, especially if you feel your actors need specific props to make the story work. Remember Shakespeare's play *Hamlet*? Remember how he holds poor Yorick's severed skull in his hand and makes a speech? In this scene, just any old prop, like a helmet or a doll's head, won't do. The scene calls for a realistic male's skull to make it authentic. The producer will be in charge of making sure that the play stays within the budget. Your input on what the show needs will help the producer set spending priorities so the play can be as authentic as possible.

Auditioning

Auditioning is the point where your play will begin to come to life. You will see people of all races, sizes, shapes, backgrounds and temperaments coming to learn what your play is all about so they can audition to become a part of the project. Even before the final role assignments are made, you'll hear different people actually reading *your* words and bringing portions of your story to life.

Since you know what you had in mind when you wrote your play, you'll want to give the producer and/or director tips and suggestions on who might be good for the roles. But be aware that your suggestions may not always be appreciated. The director may insist that this is his or her job and that your opinion isn't needed. Whatever the case, make yourself available to each actor who is auditioning and tell them what the character they're auditioning for is like.

In high school, the director is often a member of the faculty. That person will have knowledge of the talent in the school and will use that knowledge when agreeing to do your play. The director won't select your play if there aren't people in school with the talent to perform it.

Walk-Through

It's time to do a walk-through with your play's director to look for snags in the play and also to determine if what you've seen in your head can even be done on the stage. During this phase, plan to chat with the director about each scene and what you feel is needed to bring the play to life.

As you walk through and stage your play, be sure to jot down notes and details so you'll always know what works and what needs fixing. For example, maybe you've written that your main character dances

There's nothing like seeing that first "walk-through" that brings your play to life.

with a rose in his mouth, which sounds great *on paper*, but when you try this in real life, the petals drop off and your lead actor says the stem makes him want to throw up. Would you replace the actor because of the rose stem, or would you simply make a note to allow him to carry the flower in his hand?

Rehearsals

Rehearsals are usually done one of two ways or as a combination of the two: they are done as a complete read-through, where the actors read through the entire play, or they are done in a "stop and go" format, where the actor or actors work through the play one scene at a time.

Whichever way the director decides to do it, you (the playwright) should be there during rehearsals because:

1. You know this material because you wrote it. The actors and the director shouldn't have to guess what a part of the story is about; you can tell them so there will be no mistakes. According to *Play Readings: A Complete Guide for Theatre Practitioners* by Rob Urbinati, "When writers are specific about what they hope to gain, directors and actors can assist them more purposefully."
2. Since you wrote the play, you can quickly and easily answer any questions about the characters or the settings. You can tell what a character is thinking or feeling when he or she says certain things. You can also give some of the background of different characters so that the actors and director understand the characters' motivations.

3. You can offer the correct pronunciation of various names—especially if you've written a futuristic play with characters with alien-sounding names.
4. You get to hear your words come to life, and in doing so, you get to learn how well the play flows. Hopefully, everything you wanted to convey will come across. But in case it doesn't, you can take notes and decide what needs to be added, deleted, or enhanced.
5. You can listen to feedback and suggestions from the actors, who are the people who will bring your play to life. Again, what makes sense on paper may not make sense when it's being acted out. Your actors may tell you that a line "just sounds wrong" or is unbelievable. Don't dismiss this, and don't be stubborn and say, "I don't care; I'm keeping it anyway!" Don't just jump and accept it, either. Rather, take your time and think about whether what you're being told helps your story. It may make all the difference in the world.
6. You can get feedback from the director and from any other random visitors who happen to attend rehearsals. The criticism/critique may seem harsh, but you can definitely benefit from it because you will know what people are thinking and you will get to consider your play from other people's perspectives.
7. You will gain perspective on how well you get your message across. You may find that you need a bit more dialogue or you may need to stage your scenes differently. Whatever you find, you will at least understand your strengths and weaknesses as a writer, and you can go from there.
8. You can help the actors with their lines.

Off the Stage

As you have seen, there are many jobs done by people who never get near the stage. You will need to interact with them also.

You should make sure the costumers and makeup artists give each of your characters an authentic look that fits their personality in the play. If, for example, your play is set in Victorian England, you'll certainly want your actors to wear the appropriate dresses, pants, bonnets, or shoes, and your costumers will be the ones to make this happen. Or let's say you've created an incredibly shy character who can't look anyone in the eye. You may have envisioned a short character with thick glasses, a spiky haircut, and clothes that are much too big for him, so you should make sure that the costumer and makeup artist understand your vision so that your character doesn't end up with a gorgeous hairdo and the latest clothing styles. You should also work closely with the stagehands, set designers, and builders as they set up the scenery, lights, sound, props, rigging, and special effects so that they understand what you were seeing in your mind as you wrote the play.

You should also talk to the stagehands to make sure the lighting and any music chosen fit the mood of every scene. You should also let them know about requirements for sets or props so they match the time and setting of the play.

In the meantime, never forget that you are your play's first publicist. You fought for it to be understood and recognized when you placed your finished script into the hands of your teacher, director, or community playhouse staff, so you should continue to be your play's number-one cheerleader by working closely with the publicity department to be sure that absolutely everyone remains excited about it. Before the printer/graphic designer finishes the posters and flyers, you should double-check the spelling to make sure everything is perfect, then see to it that posters and flyers are set out in all the most visible places.

Publicity people can come up with creative ways to promote your play.

Last, you should work very closely with the publicity person and those responsible for sales so that tickets are distributed to a wide range of people. In fact, don't limit ticket distribution to people in your high school; hit up your local convention and visitors' bureau, too. And if your city happens to have a college or community college that teaches playwriting or theater, be sure to invite the professor so he or she can see what you've been doing.

Opening Night

Even after the set has been decorated, the play has been expertly staged, and the rehearsals are done, your presence as the playwright may still be needed for a variety of reasons. First, you may need to answer any last-minute questions the director or actors have about the characters and their motivation. It may seem surprising to you that questions may still come up at this point, but it happens. Just be sure to keep yourself at the ready.

Also make yourself available in case something happens to the person flipping the cue cards or running another sort of prompter. What could happen at this point? Plenty. The person could get sick or run late to the performance. He or she could arrive on time but forget to bring the cue cards. In this case, it would be up to you to help out with dialogue if the actors forget their lines or are temporarily stuck in the middle of dialogue.

Even if nothing this detrimental occurs, you should still be visible right up until opening night. While the director and cast members are preparing backstage, you might stand on stage and talk about your play, what inspired you to write it, and what the audience should look for as they watch. You might even answer audience questions about your writing process and your plans for the future. Of course, before you get up on stage and say anything to the audience, be sure this has been planned and you have your teacher/director's permission to do so.

Once the curtain goes up, find a seat in the back row of the auditorium or theater and watch and listen with a critical eye. Learn all you can about your own play. Learn each strength and weakness. Listen to the dialogue and watch as the actors move about onstage and deliver their lines. Determine whether you can improve your play in any way before the second performance.

That being said, remember that you are your own worst critic, and often a play isn't as bad as you (the playwright) think it is. Of course, it may not be as good as you think it is, either, but the point is to watch for the audience's reaction and try to enjoy it from a spectator's perspective. You've worked hard and you deserve it!

Juggling school and activities can seem overwhelming if you don't prioritize.

What About School Homework?

By now you are probably wondering how in the world you're going to accomplish all of the above goals and responsibilities and still manage to pass your classes and move on to the next grade. Simple: you just prioritize. Just as you have always prioritized homework assignments, home responsibilities, and extracurricular activities such as singing in the choir, playing football, or joining the debate club, you should do the same with your playwriting activity.

How? You write whenever you have time, that's how. Write whenever you have a few minutes alone, like during your lunch break. Write in the evenings after you've eaten and done your homework. Write on the weekends, too. The best times are when you have enough time to get in a groove, when you can clear your head of distractions and concentrate on your story. Once the play has been written, make sure you budget time to attend auditions, rehearsals, and any other function at which you will be needed.

Checklist: What You Should Have Learned

The preproduction part of playwriting requires just as much (or more) work as actually putting on the play before an audience.

Be open to critiques/criticism, no matter how much it hurts.

Be willing to revise/edit your script.

Stage your play alone and with the director.

Be present during auditions and rehearsals.

Keep notes on what works in your play and what doesn't.

Your job isn't over until after a successful performance has been completed. Make yourself available up until the moment the actors step out onto the stage for the first live performance.

Try to enjoy your play as a spectator and not with the critical eye of an author.

Amazing scenes like this belong on the big screen, but not on the stage.

CHAPTER FOUR

PITFALLS FOR PLAYWRIGHTS

Every job has pitfalls—even one as much fun as writing a script. As you already know, a pitfall is something unexpected, difficult, or downright dangerous that may pop up out of the blue while you're doing a job or an exercise. In theater, the pitfalls mostly center around you as the playwright, your thinking, and your aspirations. Here is a list of mistakes that playwrights like you should avoid.

Writing for Film Instead of Stage

One of the biggest mistakes newbie playwrights make is writing a script that is more like a screenplay for the movies or television than one for a play for the stage. Blogger Melissa Hillman, who writes for the *Bitter Gertrude* theater and culture blog (https://bittergertrude.com), says that many novice playwrights write micro-scenes (brief, quickly-moving scenes) that "shift back and forth from place to place, requiring a detailed set change or a massive playing space." This style of writing may be fine for the cinema, but it is nearly impossible for the theater. Here is an example of rapid scene switching:

Lights up on Kathy, who is sitting up in bed, reading a book. She suddenly puts the book down and looks sad. Lights down on Kathy and lights up on Kathy's boyfriend, Jim, who is at a crowded club dancing with an unknown girl. Lights down on Jim and his date, then lights up on Kathy's doctor's office, where her doctor is sitting behind his desk and has just received a report about Kathy's blood test. He reaches for the telephone. Lights down on the doctor's office and lights up on Kathy's mother, who is working in her garden and answers the telephone. Close-up on her face as she listens to the doctor then runs inside the house into the kitchen and splashes water on her face.

This is too many scene changes for the stage. Playwrights must be careful about these types of scripts and should also be careful about writing scenes that just don't translate to the stage, like a huge fire, a complex kung fu scene, or an angel that appears out of thin air and then flies away into the auditorium rafters.

Creating Problematic Stage Directions

Some stage directions can pose a problem if the character becomes inaudible while performing them. For example, maybe you've written a scene in which the main character walks from the back of the auditorium, down the aisle, and then up onto the stage. This is fine if he doesn't need to speak, but if your directions call for him to speak the entire time he is walking up the aisle, this may render his words hard to understand or hear. Nobody likes to strain to hear a speaker's words, but beyond that, poor sound can ruin the experience of anyone who has suffered some hearing loss. Have you ever watched a television program that looked great visually but you couldn't understand a word that the characters were saying? Annoying, wasn't it? You probably didn't wait too long before you changed the channel.

Another problematic stage direction is writing wardrobe changes that are impossible to execute. For example, let's say you've written a play about a mermaid that changes into a two-legged girl as often as she likes, and your play calls for her to constantly change back and forth. It will typically take time (and skill) for the mermaid to wriggle off of the stage (or be carried off), and then to undress and return to the audience as a two-legged girl. If it takes too long, the audience may become bored; also, if the process is too tedious, the actress may become vexed.

Thinking Your Work Is Perfect

We all like to think that we are at the top of our game and our talents shine through like the morning sun. Unfortunately, that's just not true. Becoming a good playwright is just like any other profession or job: you must practice to get better. There is no exact number of rewrites you must do before your work is the best it can be. Just prepare yourself and understand that you may have to put in a lot of work to get it just right.

Some writers take it upon themselves to write dozens of drafts before they feel their script is perfect—and even then it's not truly "perfect" because nothing ever really is. Still, they were willing to rewrite as many times as necessary to get the script just the way they wanted it. Being a good writer takes practice, and lots of it. Being willing to invest as much time and effort as is needed is what separates mediocre writers from great writers.

By the way, if your teacher, writing coach, or theater director asks you to rewrite your script, don't take it personally. Don't feel like you're a failure, and definitely don't feel that someone is out to get you. Be open minded enough to listen to the person's reasons for feeling that your play needs a bit more polishing.

Accepting Criticism

The only way to know if your work is resonating with others is to allow others to read it—and most of the time, the only way others will read it is if they know you won't get angry and retaliate if they don't like it. Accept the fact that you *must* allow your work to be critiqued in order to know what works and what doesn't.

Again, becoming a great writer takes practice, so understand that rewriting is a part of the process. One thing to keep in mind is that even after you do become a great writer, you must remain open to the thought that everyone won't like what you write or understand what you're trying to say. Some of their words may sound harsh and unnecessary, but you must force yourself to listen if your work is ever going to be better. Of course, listening and allowing

Don't let criticism or rewrites frustrate you. It's all part of the writing process.

yourself to be berated or ostracized are different things altogether.

Allowing Others to Edit Your Script

You've worked hard on your play. You've given it your all. Then suddenly, here comes a director who decides to change some of your scenes—or cut some of them out completely. Or perhaps one or more of the actors decides that the explanation you've given them about what motivates the character isn't working, so they decide to create their own motivation.

Often, a playwright doesn't have control over his or her play after it is completed. In the movie business, a final screenplay is often completely different from the way it was submitted. The same thing can happen in the theater. Once a play leaves the playwright's hands, it is the director who decides what stays in the script and what goes.

Actor Stevie Ray Dallimore is the producing director of The Muse of Fire Project, a program that listens to children and encourages them to express themselves through playwriting. Dallimore says that children are encouraged to write whatever play they want to write, with the understanding that once it's finished, it's out of their hands. Once they hand the play over to him, he says, "Okay, see you on opening night." This means the young playwrights don't know how the play flows, how the dialogue sounds, or anything else—until opening night.

No one wants their masterpiece changed, but in playwriting, it's one of those things that simply "goes with the territory."

Watching Others Ruin Your Play

Even though you have put everything you have into your play, the final production is only as good as the actors who play the characters and the director who guides them. One major pitfall is that the characters may be miscast or the director may be clueless and not understand what you were trying to say. Even a perfect script won't survive under such a scenario, but things like this do happen, especially in high school, so prepare for the possibility.

If you're tempted to make a negative comment to an actor or to the director, count to ten and then don't say anything. Why? Because negative comments don't help anyone, they only make people angry. Just as you do not want anyone saying anything negative about your play, your writing, or your talent, you should give others the same courtesy. If you absolutely must say something, make it constructive criticism. Here's an example:

Bad choice: "Jim, you're killing my character. Your acting stinks!"

Good choice: "Wow, Jim. I didn't know you were so talented. Just one thing: that character just lost his brother and is feeling really alone in this scene. I can't wait to see what you do with this scene now that you have this information."

Dealing with Negativity

When you put your work out there, you're opening yourself up for criticism—not just the criticism of your classmates or the other people in your school, but even criticism of random people who come out to see your play.

People criticize others' work for all sorts of reasons. Some don't realize they're being critical and actually think they're helping you. Others know full well they're not being helpful, but they criticize anyway because making you feel bad somehow makes them feel good.

Even though criticism can hurt, try to listen. Hear the person out to see if anything they say is actually helpful to you. If it is, count yourself lucky that someone shared a valuable tidbit of advice that actually improved your play.

If someone is being downright nasty, take a deep breath before you respond. There's no point in advising you not to take something like this personally because it is personal. It's your work.

How much more personal can it get? Still, try not to engage in an argument or debate. Just keep telling yourself, "If they could have done a better job, why didn't they? Where's their play?"

Not Taking Your Time

Writing is like every other skill in life; the more you practice, the better you get. Although you probably want to finish your play as quickly as possible so that you can see it produced, it's never a good idea to be in too big of a hurry. When you're in a hurry, you leave out important details, or your story may be inconsistent. For example, your character may have three siblings in the first part of your story, but only two in the second part because you made a change in the storyline but forgot to double-check the entire play for consistency. This is why you should take your time and think about the story you want to tell. Think about all the things you want your audience to know about your protagonist's life, hopes, dreams, and fears.

Practice telling your story aloud because this will give you a good idea of how well you know your own story and how well you can get your ideas across. How do you practice telling it aloud? Think about the last time you saw a great movie and you wanted to tell your best friend about it. Remember how you told your friend that the movie was about a boy, a girl, a doll, or whatever, and what that person or doll's life was like in the beginning? Remember telling your friend what suddenly happened to change the main character's life, and then what happened next, and what happened after that? Remember how you made sure not to tell any of the storyline out of sequence (order) because it would not have made sense if you did? And remember how you built up the tension until you got to the big finish, where you told your friend how the story ended?

That's how you practice telling your story aloud. Tell it aloud just as if you're telling your friend about a movie. Turn on a voice recorder and record yourself telling your story. Talk into the recorder in a conversational voice as if you're talking to your friend. Tell your friend everything about the story from beginning to middle to end. When you're finished, replay the recording and listen. How does the story sound? Did you lay out all the important details? Did the story make sense, or was it garbled? Will your friend react the way you expect him or her to react? If not, why? Is it because you didn't describe the story correctly?

This type of practice will help you be much clearer when you actually sit down and write. Naturally, if you don't have a recorder you can simply stand in front of a mirror and talk to your reflection as if you're talking to a friend. Whichever method you use, make a practice of telling your story so that you become more adept at getting it across to another person.

Also, challenge yourself to write an elevator speech. That's one that must be delivered before the elevator doors open. The speech answers the question, "What's your play about?" If you can't answer this question before the doors open, then you are not sure yourself. Focus on your answer, whittling it down, and you won't lose your way when writing your play.

A good public speaking class will prepare you to speak with audiences about your writing.

Take As Many Classes As You Can

As mentioned, formal classes aren't necessary to be a playwright, but it's always great if you can add a little knowledge and skill to your résumé. Consider taking a class in public speaking because it will help you overcome any fears you might have about speaking in front of audiences. It also teaches you to project your voice and physical presence, and to be a better listener. A playwright can apply the strategies learned in a public speaking class if called upon to say a few words after the play wraps up or when fielding questions while mingling with members of the audience.

Take a playwriting class if you can. Not only will such a class teach you how to turn ideas into plays, it will teach you structure, story arc, and character development, and you will also learn how to format your script should you decide to submit it to a professional theater or agent.

Take some acting classes. That's right, acting classes. Why? Because being on the acting end—having to say the words that someone else has written—will teach you how important it is to get the dialogue just right. You will, in effect, be "walking a mile in someone else's shoes."

Use Playwriting Software

Although you are not a professional at this point, it won't hurt to know how professionals format their plays for submission. Screenwriting software can be expensive, but there are free alternatives out there.

It's never too early to learn how to professionally format and submit a play.

Microsoft Office has a free screenwriting template. Just run a search in your favorite search engine and you'll find it.

Celtx (https://www.celtx.com/index.html) is a free software that has mobile and desktop versions that sync up well with cloud services. If you don't know what all this means, don't worry, you don't have to. As long as you have a computer, tablet, or some other way to access it on the internet, you should be good to go. Special Note: Even though Celtx is free, it requires you to sign up before you can

ALMOST, MAINE

John Edward Cariani is a man of many talents. He played a forensic expert named Julian Beck on the series *Law & Order*, and he earned a Tony Award nomination for his role (Motel the Tailor) in a Broadway revival of *Fiddler on the Roof*. However, despite his television and theater accolades, Mr. Cariani is best known as the author of *Almost, Maine*, a play with nine two-character vignettes (episodes) that are "all about falling in and out of love in a remote town called Almost, Maine." At least one vignette tells the story of two young men in love, though, according to Mr. Cariani, "not sexual love."

Almost, Maine premiered at the Portland Stage Company (Portland, Maine) and broke box office records and garnered critical acclaim soon after. It then opened Off-Broadway on January 12, 2006, but closed a month later in February of 2006. Even so, the play had already made an impact and was soon featured as one of the "best plays in 2006" in Smith and Kraus Publishers' *New Playwrights: Best Plays of 2006*. It was also named "one of the ten must-see shows" in the *Wall Street Journal*'s regional roundup (2004–2005).

Playwright is one of John Edward Cariani's titles.

Somewhere along the way, *Almost, Maine* became a high school theater favorite. It is currently the "most produced play in North American high schools," surpassing *A Midsummer Night's Dream*, by William Shakespeare.

have a local community theater, ask for their schedule and seat pricing. Also ask if you can attend free or at a reduced price because you are an emerging playwright.

If your city has a community college, check to see if it offers theater classes. If it does, ask the instructor if you can audit (attend without the benefit or goal of receiving a grade) some of the classes, staged readings, or actual productions. If you explain that you are a high school student who is trying to learn, you may even be paired up with other playwrights in the community college class so you can get hands-on experience about the life of a playwright.

If all else fails, visit Youtube.com, Vimeo.com, or some other video platform and watch as many plays as you can find.

Engage with Other Playwrights

There's almost nothing better than finding people who love the same things you love—especially when it comes to writing plays. When you meet someone with similar interests, you get the chance to learn about that person's technique, discuss your own work, and bounce around ideas about staging, characterization, and getting your play produced.

How do you find that person or persons? There are many organizations that celebrate young playwrights. To find them, type "Opportunities for young playwrights" in your favorite search engine and browse until you find something that sparks your interest. One of the most visible organizations you'll probably find is called Young Playwrights (http://www.youngplaywrights.org), which was founded by Stephen Sondheim. It accepts plays from playwrights ages eighteen and younger who are still enrolled in school. Even if you're not ready to submit a play, you may be able to communicate with one of the administrators via a website contact form and ask for suggestions on how you can find other young playwrights like yourself.

Another way to find other young playwrights is by attending different writers' conventions. You might get your local community theater to help you find relevant conventions or workshops where you can meet other young writers. Just keep in mind that many of these workshops can be pricey to attend, but they're usually worth it.

Try searching Facebook or other social networks to see if there are "rooms" for young writers. If there are not, you may want to consider creating a room (it's free, after all!) and then soliciting others to join.

If you're lucky, there will be many young playwrights in your city that you can talk to and share ideas with. However, this isn't always the case, so it may be challenging to find a compatible young playwright that you can share your journey with. In this case, try to find an adult playwright who lives nearby and see if you can "shadow" him or her. "Shadowing" means that you'll attend certain meetings or rehearsals with your mentor, go to luncheons or attend staged readings with him or her, etc., to see first-hand what being a playwright involves. Try your local community college or community theater, if you have one. You'll find that the theater community is typically very generous and is always willing to assist an aspiring playwright.

One of the pitfalls of live theater is people being unintentionally rude.

Rules of Etiquette

The word "etiquette" means "a customary code of polite behavior in society or among the members of a particular group." Schools, churches, hospitals, ballparks—all of these have rules of etiquette. The theater has rules of etiquette, too.

Writer, director, and actor Charles Patterson of Christal Entertainment has been working with both adults and children in the theater for many years. According to Patterson, there is a code of conduct in the theater, and not just for the audience. Almost everyone knows that the audience is expected to get to the theater on time and turn off all cell phones when the play begins. They should not talk during the performance or snap photos that may temporarily blind the cast members. They also shouldn't throw anything onstage or boo certain cast members while they cheer for others. These are all hard and fast rules of etiquette for the audience members.

But what about rules for the cast members? Patterson has some great rules. "I tell my actors that no matter what they see or hear from the audience, to just keep going," he says. "And once the house [theater] is open, [I tell them to] stay off the stage and out of sight. Don't mingle with friends, family, or the waiting audience before the show."

Here are some of Patterson's other tips about theater etiquette that can apply to the playwright:

1. The director and/or the stage manager are the only ones who can give notes or direction to cast members; nobody else.
2. Constructive criticism is always welcome.
3. Never touch someone else's props or their costumes.
4. Do not use mobile telephones when behind the stage; you could become a distraction.
5. Always be respectful of everyone you work with: directors, staff, **crew**, and designers.
6. Make sure you arrive on time so that you don't interfere with the play, and remain **offstage**.

The Show Must Go On

The phrase "The show must go on" means that no matter what happens before or on opening night (or any other night that the play is performed), the show that has been planned and publicized *must* be performed for the waiting audience. No excuses.

What kinds of things can happen that can affect the show? The lead actor could come down with laryngitis, or one or more of the cast members could break out in measles. The stagehands could get stuck in traffic on opening night, or a terrible electric storm could knock out power. The sound system could fail, or the auditorium roof might be leaking after yesterday's rain. Someone onstage could stub a toe or get hit by a prop, or the school's or auditorium's fire alarm could go off and everyone may have to evacuate the building.

The point is not so much that these sorts of things happen; the point is that you and the cast members should always be prepared just in case something does happen. For example, if the cue card person mistakenly leaves the cue cards at home on the coffee table, you can be the cue person because you know the material better than anyone. If the lead actor has laryngitis, you can help prepare the understudy to fill the void. If the fire alarm sounds, encourage everyone to evacuate the building as quickly as possible, but direct them to wait until the firemen give the all clear so that you can finish the play once you go back inside. Be prepared to help in any situation.

Whatever you do, try to remain level headed and calm on opening night and other performance nights. Always remember that anything can happen, and try to be prepared so that if the play does get off track, you can help usher it back on track without too much disruption.

Playwriting gives you lots of tools you can use when you're ready to get a real job.

CHAPTER FIVE

PLAYWRITING ROLES AND THE REAL WORLD

As with just about everything, experience brings about a world of opportunity. Although you don't necessarily need experience to write a play, getting some experience under your belt won't hurt. In fact, it will probably help things go more smoothly, and you will gain some important life skills in the process.

What can theater experience do for you? Here are just a few things it can do for your personal growth.

Build Your Self-Confidence: Are you shy about your work? Are you worried about speaking in front of others? These worries won't last long when you participate in the theater. First, if your play got accepted, that should help your self-confidence. As a playwright, your work is going to be read by many people, including the director, the producer and all the actors; and it's going to be viewed by many others, including your family and friends, the actors' families and friends, and random strangers in the audience. Being constantly "under the microscope" this way will help you become accustomed to the scrutiny of others, and their praise and appreciation will boost your confidence.

Theater puts you in contact with people with different interests and outlooks.

Expand Your Horizons: As you meet other playwrights (online or via live networking) and read their plays, you will get an introduction to the lives that other young people live. You will see that the world is a big place with all types of personalities, talents, experiences, and skin colors. This will increase your cultural awareness and promote acceptance for others who may not live like you live, read what you read, or believe the things you believe.

Prepare You for Your Next Script: Whenever you learn a new skill, the first time is usually the most challenging. Once you've completed the routine a time or two, things usually proceed smoothly and without too much difficulty. The same goes for writing scripts. The first time you write a script, coming up with a great idea, organizing it, writing and perfecting a script, and getting the story you want to tell across may seem next to impossible. Once you learn what to do first, how to organize your thoughts, and how to structure your play, writing your next play should be much less daunting. This will happen even if your first efforts are rejected. This doesn't mean that your second play will be accepted; it only means that actually brainstorming, writing, revising, and completing your play will feel like second nature to you.

Increase Opportunities: If you possess a gift or a talent, and if others know about it, you will be asked to use it more often. In this case, if you write one play, your teachers, family, and friends will probably ask you to write an introduction for the next event or an article for the school newspaper. They may even watch for other writing opportunities for you and then pass these along so you don't miss out.

Improve Academic Performance: According to the American Alliance for Theatre and Education, "Students who participate in drama often experience improved reading comprehension, maintain better attendance records, and stay generally more engaged in school than their non-arts counterparts."

Sharpen Verbal Skills: Writing lines for actors and then listening to and critiquing them as they deliver these lines should help to sharpen your verbal

AN EARLY START

In 2012, a Sarasota, Florida, third grader named Spencer Emerson Opal-Levine wrote a play titled *Coffee Talk* about a coffee bean that wanted to be more than just a mere coffee bean, and he ended up as one of twelve winners of the Blank Theatre's Young Playwrights Festival of Hollywood, California. The theater's artistic producer is none other than actor Noah Wyle of *ER* fame. In Spencer's play, coffee beans hang out in a coffee shop and chat about what they want to be. One bean wants to be a latte, one dreams of being a dry roast, but one very special bean wants to be different: he wants to become coffee ice cream. His preference shocks the other beans, but they soon admire his originality.

The then nine-year-old Spencer was the youngest winner ever of the Blank Theatre's Young Playwrights Festival. Adam Ratner, coordinator of the Florida Studio Theater's Young Playwrights Festival, told the Sarasota *Herald-Tribune* that the play is "an allegory about being yourself and [doing] what makes you happy." Spencer has gone on to write and receive honors and recognition for other plays, including *Sox* (the story of a sock that gets separated from its partner), which also was among the winners at the Blank Theatre's Young Playwrights Festival in 2013. It was performed twice during Kids Day at the County Fair in Morgantown, West Virginia. One of the cast members was John Farley, brother of the late Chris Farley. *Sox* earned Spencer the title of "Youngest winner of the 10-Minute Play Festival at M.T. Pockets."

performance scores—especially since you may need to deliver the lines yourself to demonstrate what the scenes should be like.

Increase Comprehension: Breaking down a play (like one of Shakespeare's masterpieces) or breaking down your own for others and sharing the interpretation and the meaning behind the dialogue can lead to a better understanding of language and text.

Sharpen Listening Skills: Since you wrote the play and you know how the dialogue should be spoken, you'll find yourself listening carefully as the rehearsals progress. This act of listening should sharpen your personal skills.

Increase Your Literary Knowledge: As you check out more books on the subject of playwriting—and as you watch videos and/or network with other young playwrights, your literary knowledge should expand accordingly.

Professional Benefits

There is so much to learn in the world of theater and playwriting. For example, did you know that onstage theater jobs can help to prepare you for jobs off the stage? It's true; the skills you learn in order to be successful in the theater can also serve you well outside of the theater.

As a playwright, you weave a story and tell it via both verbal (dialogue) and nonverbal expression. The nonverbal expression includes what you write about

You can parlay your playwriting talent into teaching positions.

the way the characters will move and interact, the costumes they wear, the setting, and even the music you suggest for the production. As you tweak your skills in verbal and nonverbal expression, you will find that they can be carried beyond the theater. You can use these storytelling skills in public libraries; in elementary, middle or high school classrooms; in the professional theater; behind the scenes of a television studio; or even on a movie set. These are all broad examples, but there are dozens more writing jobs that can evolve from your beginnings as a playwright. Here are a few specific examples, in no particular order:

Producer: Since the playwright's and the producer's job can overlap, producer or "production manager" is a great job for a playwright to transition into. The producer (or production manager) is responsible for finding great plays to perform and seeing to it that the entire production (the play) is performed within budget and at the agreed-upon time. This person knows the script inside and out, and determines the budget, the target audience, and where and when the play will be performed. He or she keeps an eye on the budget, conducts meetings with cast and crew, and develops a marketing plan or strategy for getting all the work done. This budgeting, financing, scheduling, and marketing experience should carry over well into other settings, too, including management (like in fast-food restaurants settings where employees must be scheduled in shifts), project management (where you work in tandem with creative and business people), and even in human resource departments.

Producer's Assistant/Script Reviewer: Even if you don't become a producer, you may consider becoming a producer's assistant. Producers are often so busy that they just don't have time to read all the scripts that are submitted for consideration. In this case, it would be your job to read the scripts, weed out the bad or boring ones, then chat with the producer about those that are "possibilities."

Advertising Copywriter: By the time you are ready to get a job, you will probably have gained much experience in writing lines that attract and hold an audience's attention. You may have even written stage directions that keep your audience engaged. In this case, you may want to consider becoming an entry-level advertising copywriter. This person writes advertising and product descriptions for email campaigns and print and online catalogs. They may also write scripts for commercials or online campaigns.

Writer-in-Residence: Colleges and universities recruit accomplished authors as writers-in-residence to live at or near their campuses for a period of time. The writer usually gets room and board free in exchange for teaching a class or mentoring one or more young people. A job like this would allow you to travel to new places, work at something you love, and be fed and paid for doing it.

Arts Fundraiser: This is a position for a person who is expected to reach out to the community and persuade them to donate funds to a certain endeavor. In this case, that endeavor may be as narrow as the theater or as broad as the category of "personal creativity."

Author: If you're writing original plays, you're already an author. However, you may want to go one step further and try your hand at writing short stories, novellas, and novels. Just keep in mind that writing and publishing can be a lengthy process, so it may require you to find other work while you pursue your passion.

Blogger: Almost everyone blogs these days, and although there are not many people making a decent living off of blogging, you may be able to if you use your imagination. There are lots of theater websites out there. There are also many successful scriptwriters. These companies and individuals may be so busy that they have no time to post to their sites, and that's where you come in. You may be able take care of their social and personal blogging needs, and learn something from them in the process.

Dramaturge: The professional dramaturge does all the editing, writing, researching, and advising in a theater production. He or she analyzes the script or story that is to be performed and makes detailed notes for the director. The dramaturge may also be the one who writes the audience "guide" to the play.

Ghostwriter: Ghostwriters are writers who write stories or scripts for pay. Typically, the employer (the one who wants something written) will already have a topic in mind. In many cases, he or she even has an outline and list of topics to cover. In this case, it would be your job to simply write the script or story for an agreed-upon amount and then turn the finished product over to the employer. The pros are that you'll gain experience and you'll be paid for what you write. However, the cons are that you will have to sign a nondisclosure form (a form where you vow that you will never divulge the fact that you are the writer), and you'll never be acknowledged as the writer, even if what you've written turns into a runaway bestseller.

Scriptwriter: Since you've already written a play or are at least in the process, you understand the basics of what a scriptwriter does. In this position you would probably write scripts for movies, cartoons, or local or national TV shows.

Theater Educator: Once you've garnered enough experience in theater, you may want to become a theater coach. According to "Theatre Major Career Guide," theater educators "coach students in the techniques of acting, directing, playwriting, script analysis, and the history of theatre. They help students acquire confidence, assurance, speaking

With additional credentials, you may be able to coach youths in creative expression.

skills, and timing. They encourage students in their work, direct rehearsals, and guide them in their roles. At the same time, they instruct students in backstage work including set design, production organization, set building, stage lighting and sound, properties, costuming, and makeup."

There are many more writing jobs out there. You could write children's books, television skits, game scripts, graphic novel scripts, or video scripts. You could interview people who write scripts, or you could write flyers, user manuals, or web copy. And because you now have experience writing plays, you could write a book on how to write plays.

Writers For Hire

"Theatre Major Career Guide" also offers an interesting list of the organizations that often hire theater majors or those with theater experience.

This list includes community organizations, theaters, fundraising firms, television studios, libraries, cruise lines, colleges, amusement parks, film companies, and performing arts organizations.

Check out the following online articles to get a sense of where your writing career can take you:

Melissa Donovan posted the story "20 Creative Writing Careers" on her *Writing Forward* blog in 2014. Find it at http://www.writingforward.com/creative-writing/creative-writing-careers.

Blogger John Hewitt posted the "Glossary of Writing Careers" in 2014. Find it at http://www.poewar.com/glossary-of-writing-careers.

Kimberly Pendergrass posted "Writing Careers That You Have Probably Never Thought Of" on the *udemy* blog in 2013. Find it at https://blog.udemy.com/writing-careers.

Great Adventure

Becoming a playwright and being involved in the theater is a multifaceted adventure that has many pluses. You get to see your creative dreams brought to life, and you acquire some very important life skills in the process, including teamwork, brainstorming, writing, organizing, self-expression, and meeting deadlines. Whatever your goals, just remember to enjoy the journey along the way.

GLOSSARY

adaptation A movie, television drama, or stage play that is based on a written work, typically a novel.

ad lib To speak or perform in public without previously practicing or preparing your words; in a play, going off script.

antagonist The person in the play who actively opposes or is hostile to someone or something, usually the hero or main character.

backstory A history or a background that is created for a fictional character.

blocking To move or position actors for the best dramatic effect and to tell the story in visual form.

brainstorming When a group of people meet to generate new ideas around a specific area of interest.

character A person in a narrative work, such as a novel, play, television series, or film.

climax The high point or most important part of a plot.

comedy A style of a movie, play, or broadcast program that is intended to make an audience laugh.

conflict Any obstacle that gets in the way of a character achieving whatever it is that he or she wants the most. This is what the character struggles against.

creative writing A form of artistic expression in which the author draws on his or her imagination to give meaning to a situation through imagery, drama, and narrative.

crew Workers whose job it is to move scenery or handle properties in a theatrical production.

denouement The resolution of the conflict in a plot.

dialogue A conversation between two or more people.

falling action The series of events following the climax of a plot.

full-length play Plays that are sometimes called "evening-length plays" because they are typically seventy or eighty minute plays—long enough to last a whole evening.

improvisation A form of live theater where the plot, characters, and dialogue of a game, scene, or story are made up on the spot.

monodrama A dramatic or musical piece that is played by a single actor or singer, usually portraying one character.

monologue A speech presented by a single character to the audience. It can also refer to a lengthy address to another character.

offstage Not on the stage but in the wings and not visible to the audience.

one-act play A play that constitutes only one act and isn't long enough to constitute a full evening.

playwright A person who writes plays.

plot The structure of a play, including exposition, rising action, climax, falling action, and denouement.

protagonist The leading character (or one of the major characters) in a drama, movie, novel, or other text.

publicity person The person given the task of spreading awareness of your play, often without paying for it.

real time When events are portrayed at the same rate at which the characters experience them.

setting The time and place of a scene.

shadowing In theater, in school, or at work, this is

when you follow someone around to learn about a particular occupation or way of doing something. It is usually an educational activity.

sketch A short, humorous play or performance, consisting typically of one scene in a comedy program.

tag Sometimes called a "character tag," it is something (a look, a physical characteristic, a sound like a nasally voice) that you use repeatedly with a character to make it easy for readers or audience members to identify them.

ten-minute play A complete, compact play, with a beginning, middle, and end, in which the story takes place in one scene and runs no more than ten pages (each page represents one minute in time).

ticket sales The financial lifeblood of the theater, this is the selling of a guaranteed seat in the house for a play either in advance or at the theater on the night of the performance.

FOR MORE INFORMATION

Books

Bentley, Nancy, and Donna Guthrie. *Putting on a Play: The Young Playwright's Guide to Scripting, Directing, and Performing*. Minneapolis, MN: The Millbrook Press, 1996

Dorf, Jonathan. *Young Playwrights 101: A Practical Guide For Young Playwrights and Those Who Teach Them*. Burbank, CA: YouthPlays Press, 2005.

Neipris, Janet. *To Be a Playwright*, New York: Routledge, 2005.

Young Playwrights' Theater. *2015 New Play Festival (Volume 4)*. Washington, DC: Young Playwrights' Theater, 2015.

Online Articles

McGiven, Erik Sean. "Blocking and Movement." ErikSeanMcGiven.com. http://www.erikseanmcgiven.com/writings/acting/blocking-and-movement/

Websites

American Association of Community Theatre

http://www.aact.org

This association assists community theater groups through a variety of methods, and its website includes links that can help young playwrights.

Blank Theatre Company

http://www.youngplaywrights.com

The website of the Blank Theater Young Playwrights Festival provides information on this formative writing competition.

Center Stage

http://www.centerstage.org

This professional theater in Baltimore, Maryland, provides an educational section that includes information on writing competitions, study guides, and articles such as "Teaching Playwriting in Schools."

Theatre Folk

https://www.theatrefolk.com

This site is a great resource for young playwrights. You can find links to helpful books and blog posts, such as one titled "Preparing for the First Day of Rehearsal—A Guide for Student Actors."

Young Playwrights Inc.

http://www.youngplaywrights.org

Stephen Sondheim founded this organization that seeks to identify, develop, and promote playwrights under the age of eighteen. It holds an annual writing contest.

INDEX

Page numbers in **boldface** are illustrations. Entries in **boldface** are glossary terms.

ABOUT THE AUTHOR

Rita Lorraine Hubbard is a retired educator and full-time author and researcher of fiction and nonfiction. She founded TheBlackHistoryChannel.com and PictureBookDepot.com, both of which enjoy a global audience. She earned East Tennessee's Community History Award (2014), SCBWI's 2014 Letter of Merit, and Lee and Low Books' 2012 New Voices Award. She is also the author of *African Americans of Chattanooga: A History of Unsung Heroes*, and several other educational titles.